DEEP AUGUST

poems

by

Jessica Isaacs

ISBN: 978-1-936923-10-6

First Edition 2014

Cover Art & Design by Devey Napier

Village Books Press Cheyenne, Oklahoma

Special thanks to Rayshell Clapper, Dorothy Alexander, Devey Napier, Ken Hada, and Michael Isaacs for their time and help in the editing, revision and cover art of this book. Their honesty and careful attention to detail are truly priceless.

Acknowledgments:
Several of the poems in this book have been published in other journals and anthologies, most recently including *Cybersoleil, Sugarmule,* and *Elegant Rage.*
isclaimer:l of the poems in this book are works of the poet's imagination. All of the persons and events depicted are fiction. Any resemblance to actual persons or events is purely coincidental.

smoldering embers

poetry is forged
by the slow burn of Life and
the hammer of Time

for my family and their time

Table of Contents

Part One – Seductive Branches

Part Two – Our Shadows into the Sky

Part Three – She Dreamed of Running

seductive branches

Sumac

red and purple jewels,
the poison sumac beckons,
seductive branches

wind along with me

on these curves of tortoise shells creeping
through this desert and the soft dunes stirred effortlessly
by sidewinders gliding across the sand,
on these curves of snowflakes mounding in drifts
along rows of quiet houses, on these curves
of cinnamon rolls rising in ovens, on these curves
of smoke billowing into us from our morning coffee,
on these curves of my hand brushing your cheek resting
on our down pillows in your first moments of waking,
on these curves of my gray hair falling across your comforting lap
in the summer nights, on these curves
of bare feet, round heels and high arches, silkily tiptoeing
down winding beach paths through windswept grasses,
on these curves of naked calves and rounded breasts rising
to greet the pull of the round, round moon, on these curves
of waves cresting to break upon rounded whales' backs rising
higher than mountains, plunging deeper than infinity, looping
backwards and forwards and always onwards into you, into me,
knotting our lives together on these winding roads of years
and pulsing promises of yes, yes, yes,
billowing our moments upon these curves
of buxom dandelions,   *ritardando*
soaring our spirits
into clouds

Air

Their lust
was as natural as air,
and like air,
she could not see
it, could not contain
it, but simply felt
his presence enveloping
her, pervading
her . . .

He
was the Montana night sky
that she could smell,
the quiet
she could taste.

He
was the Aurora Borealis
          – electrifying –
all the world below him
          – stirring –
the wolves to awaken
          – compelling –
them to howl
their wild nightsongs . . .

Who
     could deny
         air?

River-bottom Boy

Sweet Oklahoma river-bottom boy,
we sank our feet in the silt of years
built up in the sandbar,
we let our passion run wild
and sure like the current,
sometimes almost drowning
ourselves in its undertow, struggling
to come up for air, knocking
against the rocks of lost jobs, sick babies
stacks of bills, dishes, and delayed dreams,
surfacing only briefly, gasping
for breath, only to be swept away again,
carried away
in the current of our lives,
secure in nothing
but the surety, the swiftness of the river –
the intensity
of the rapids, the religion of the water –
our faith placed in the knowledge
that all rivers flow
toward a greater place,
our hope in believing
that all rivers lead
home.

You

are the stars in my sky,
fireflies in my summer nights,

You
are the heat
of my July dreams

One Summer Night,

you kissed my neck, and I trembled –
you knew you could make me do
whatever you wanted –
so you took my hand, and led me out
into the backyard at night,
under the oak leaves, under the bats swooping down
to feed on the swarming mosquitoes . . .

"Come on, baby, let's do it on the trampoline,"
you whispered in my hair,
pulling my clothes off, leading me, barefoot,
across the grass . . .

until . . .

splat!

I stepped in dog shit,
and you handed me back
my shirt.

Draco

These people who dare to love poets,
they must be both sadist and masochist alike,
they must delight in dancing with the dragon,
must thrill themselves with biting and scratching
and stabbing the dragon into a ferocious fury,
until the dragon's breath melts the lovers in their passion,
the dragon-poet's forked tongue flicking out
from between its bared teeth, lapping at the lovers' blood,
their promises, their squeals of pained delight, licking up
their salty needs in a scaly, feeding frenzy until the glutted dragon
slinks back into the deepest bowels of the earth,
the abandoned lovers left shivering naked on the rocks
in the inevitable coldness of the cave –
ah! these people who dare to love poets,
they must revel
in the sharpest ice   ] *ritardando*
of home.

13

Burnished

Your words fall in beads across my body
like drops of oil in water,
falling across my temples, gliding across my neck,
my shoulders, my arms, my breasts,

soothing the deep, aching burns ,
left in the creases of my hands
from holding on too tightly
to my security like a rope;

your acceptance rippling
across my thighs; your forgiveness healing
the cracks left in my heels and soles
from treading too long at the volcano's edge;

your unwavering love and desire
showering me in a dazzling eruption
of luminescent droplets –
oil like light on my hair, on my skin –

burnishing me.

Toilet Redemption

I strain to hear the weatherman
over my stream of urine
and a closed door.

Storms may meet you on the road.
I hate to think of you traveling so far,
so long, so late, with weather.

I call to you to stay, don't chance driving
in bad conditions; besides, there is something else
I want you to know.

I stand and open the door.
I'll tell it to you frankly;
this is no love poem.

I make no fancy confessions, but simply
flush the toilet and pick up the novel
I thought I might need.

This is an honest dedication, plain, no frills,
like your burgers, meat and bread only,
but just as satisfying, just as necessary.

You are the furniture in my shambled house,
the couch that catches me,
the lamp spilling a small spot-circle of light;

all this I need.

You are my toilet, swallowing my shit
and forever rinsing me clean.

Acid

once, I dreamed of you – the ghost
of your youthful passion –
but now, you are nothing

but the night air –
thin and fleeting – you
are nothing –

but a smoldering apparition,
like acid in my core –
and I learn to sleep

with the blackened char
of crumbling dreams of you –
I learn to believe

that you are nothing
but a leftover childhood –

a lingering ghost

Guardian

1   The pyramids of Giza rise
out of the heat of the Earth, shameless
under the ancient sun, radiant
with the energy of the ages, wisdom
5   of worlds gone by, guardians
of secrets buried deep within –
sacred, dark centers buried deep within.

Mysteries unearthed, treasures exposed, *This is her.*
secrets exploited for tourists' delights;
10   sun scorching, heat exacting *This is life*
the same tribute now as then, and I
am like a guarding pyramid, built
around a secret buried deep within
the cool, still recesses of my soul.

15   Buried, hidden, mysteries no sunlight can expose
nor any lover exploit, mummified
within my heart, a perfect preservation
of your youth . . . decaying
even now, yet slowed somehow
20   out of reach of the heat and the sun,
out of reach of all knowledge.

If I unearth you, if I unwrap you, allow
the heat and the sun and the world
to see the mysteries of my pyramid –
25   you will blow away, like the dust
you are – finally formless – released
from your wrappings – finally
free from my entrapping heart –

and I, with no rights in the matter,
30   holding on to a memory, a mummy,
I preserved for my own pleasure,
to preserve a part of me – destroying
parts of both of us in the process.
Now the unveiling is harsh but natural.

35 Now the trappings fall away, revealing
what we knew was there all along; revealing
not the beauty of youth, but the ugliness
of too much time passed –
burned away – by the rising and setting
40 of many suns, by the swelling and dying
of many moons, in this, the cold winter of exposure,

when the moon has replaced
the sun at last, and the secrets –
resurrected – fulfill
the ancient curses, the ancient rhythms
that breathed alive in the sand, in the heat,
in the burning world – threatening
to consume all life, all love, all passion . . .

but like the flooded Nile, the moon pulls
our passion with its current, cooling
us now, stirring the air, turning
our trappings to dust, leaving
only a slowly decaying body to treasure – its youth
preserved cruelly in the turn of the lips,
the set of the jaw –

for the eyes melted away years ago.

Like the Scent of Sycamore

The wind whispered through the sycamores today,
and I smelled the sky, like your cologne;
you were the air on my skin, in my hair,
filling me with your breath.

The wind sighed through the sycamores today,
and I wondered why I always sensed
more was coming, like a storm threatening,
hanging heavy in swollen clouds.

The wind wailed through the sycamores today,
and I trembled at the sound,
my ears straining for your voice,
your absence a fresh grief pressing down on me,
the air humid, tense with my longing,

for, like the scent of sycamore,
your spirit hangs,
heavy, in my life.

Reaching

The skeleton-white tree
reaches her limbs to heaven
out of the red Oklahoma landscape
like a woman's slender hand
arching up to clutch
her lost lover.

Carry Me

Carry me home when I fall.
Cover me with your promises
in the cold January nights;
rock me to sleep
when the March winds drive me crazy;
tell me you love me;
carry me home.

Hold my hand when my child screams;
hold my head when my parents die.
Carry me, Love,
when my knees
won't hold me up anymore.
Carry me home.

When the hard freeze comes,
and the ice takes over at last,
carry me, Love;
bring the quilts to our bed,
kiss my forehead, tell me you love me,
tell me good night,
lay me gently in the ground,
and carve your name in my headboard.

Bring me flowers in the springtime;
remember my favorites;
lay the red Indian paintbrushes at my head.
Tell me again all the reasons why you love me;
remind me that you're coming home,
soon, dear, so very soon,
and I will rest beside you,
once again.

The Mortician's Wife

She awoke when his phone rang
at two. a.m., and reached for him
as he walked out the door for work.

Another call, another family in need . . .
another lonely night and Saturday for her . . .
she rolled over to his empty side of the bed and sighed,

pretending he was still with her.
When she can't have him, she lay in the warmth
he leaves behind.

Darkling Requiem

I sank into your death like the March rain
soaking the dry winter garden that would not be quenched.
I waited for you to come home, but the door never opened,
and the shadow of your strong shoulders
remained silhouetted only in my spirit.

Nights I reached for you broke into the dawn
of an endless expanse of a new empty infinity, and I obsessed
about the silk of my pre-arranged casket, the stillness and end
that my own death promised. [I craved you
from the other side of this black hole.]

Life, they call it.
Hell, what does the world know
about life?

> *"To take into the air my quiet breath,*
> *Now more than ever, seems it rich to die,"*

Keats' nightingale calls out to me in my dusky existence,
my requiem carries me closer to you
on the moon-soft wind of my longing,
leaving this dead, lonely existence behind
with the molted feathers of my life –

Welcome, Midnight.
Welcome, Ecstasy.

The Truck

It was the first time in months they'd had any time at all to themselves, without the kids for once on a Friday night, without somebody sick or having to work late, without being too flat broke to afford to go anywhere or do anything, without having to mow, or do seven loads of laundry, or without being too worn out to care.

He opened the door for her to their old Dodge pickup truck, helped her inside. She buckled her seatbelt, and watched him settle into the driver's seat across the bench from her, watched his shoulders flex under his shirt, watched how the muscles in his long arms still stretched and made her ache to touch them, to slide her lips across them . . . and she saw the expanse between his seat and hers – remembered how twenty years ago, she always rode the hump right next to him in this same truck . . .

Now, the distance lay between them like the years of new trucks they never bought, roads they never traveled . . . and the scenery of the seasons they simply existed alongside each other flew through her mind . . . all the time they lost, so busy spinning orbits around each other just to keep their universe in motion, using all their momentum to keep moving forward, always moving forward, like they were moving forward even now, together in this truck as old as their marriage, and both hurting for some much-overdue maintenance.

She must have seemed to him, just then, like a sensor in a motor, signaling her need for repair, for all it took was his long arm, reaching across the seat's great divide to her, one gentle stroke of her neck, steering her like he steered the wheel.

She unclicked her seatbelt, and slid across to nestle under his arm as he drove them down the old country roads, the expanse of years between them disappearing like the distance on the bench seat, and all that mattered was his arm, long and warm, sliding across her skin, pulling her to him like he did so many years ago, the dust of past and future billowing in cloudy orbits behind them, as they drove time away for the present . . . just a guy and a girl, sitting too close together in an old, beat-up, pickup truck.

Hollow

She spoke out from the broken place with the hollow of her voice:

"Because if you miss his game again, I can't,"

she said simply to her husband,
and she left him and the children all eating breakfast
so she could drive to work.

There had been a time when she picked up
all of their broken pieces, compulsively dusting them off
and arranging them neatly on the shelf of their marriage,
their family, their lives, gluing them all back together
with whatever sticky substance she could find –

always on the shelf, on the shelf, on the shelf –

but now she just let those pieces fall, and she sat down
in the middle of all of their broken shards,
wrapped herself in her blanket, and rocked and hummed
until she couldn't hear them crying after her
anymore.

Married with Kids

We lost a decade
in one fell swoop,
sort of like
the ten-years' war
of Troy.

Kitchen Moths

She faced the dark kitchen window,
and stared out into the night,
watching the moths harass the streetlight.
Dishes crusted over in the sink,

laundry spoiled in the washing machine.
She could hear her sleeping children
coughing and kicking against their sheets,
their legs restless as the crying crickets in the yard.

She tried to remember a time when she had existed
in a realm outside her everyday obligations,
but the air in her kitchen was thick, was stifling . . .
so she walked out,

into the night, under the streetlight,
her nightgown hanging onto her bare legs like a lover,
fluttering white against her darkness,
like the summer moths.

Image of a Country Commodity

wildflowers—
dying captives
of a tin can

Snowflakes in August

When you said you were going to Houston,
who was I to say no?
It was August, but in my memory,
snowflakes fell all around you –
your eyes the color of ice
searching mine for some answer –
but who was I then, and who am I now
to you, that I should have said no?

We sat in your car. I saw your hands
grip the steering wheel. I saw your forehead
wrinkle with wanderlust. I heard your voice
strain with your question – and I knew then
that you weren't ready for me yet –
but who was I then, and
who am I now to say so?
Now what I need to say is this:

When you left me for Houston,
snowflakes covered your tracks,
and no August sun since
has ever melted that ice.

White dandelions,

stripped of their seeds in the wind,
shiver, bare, exposed,
unprotected in the sun,
naked in the August heat.

snowshine and moonglow —

Winter's soft apology
for spurning the Sun

On Marriage

I.
Sixty years ago,
she graced his life with her truth,
said, "I do, Love, and
I will, Love, do my duty,
give you all my life."

II.
His fragile forgiveness is
the balance beam of her life.
Daily, she walks his lines,
focusing intensely, struggling
not to fall from grace.

III.
Climb stairs with crutches,
to learn about commitment
and fragile passion.

Just Another Archetype

Am I your river or your demon?
What renewal washes upon you from my currents,
my rock bottom scraping your ankles, my rapids
swallowing your security, threatening your life as you know it,
rushing to an unknown fall of furious freedom, plunging
into the deeps of a wild expanse and sudden calm
and sudden storm, and a new system of signals
for approaching storms and threats on these open waters,
a new captain
to fend off pirates?

I am the stowaway in your life,
your damsel in distress,
your lady in the tower,
your ripe fruit.

Cut my skin with your teeth,
pierce my flesh,
chew me slowly,
and then spit me out
into this swollen river.

You
are my demon.

Rejection
a response to Matthew Arnold's "Dover Beach"

I hear you say
the Sea of Faith
was once complete for you,
that once you trusted me beyond a doubt,
but that I let you down.
You blame me
for some pain I put you through.
I never promised love.
I never promised anything, so drown
in self-pity,
I'll do without.

You ask me
to be true to you,
and I am.

Your world to me seems
a lonely, hellish nightmare,
not a dream,
and I will never
fall in love with you,
neither sacrifice independence
nor joy of life, nor
faith in human goodness,
just to gain
a barren, desert life
you'll fill with pain.

I leave you here
to wallow in your strife.
I am a woman,
not a martyred wife.

Dragon, Bull, Shark

I am a dragon,
scaly, brilliant, breathing fire,
apt to erupt at any moment,
best left to seethe alone in my cave
where I can't hurt anyone with my passions,
scald anyone with too much joy or too much
sadness or too much pain or anger.

I am a bull,
my horns sharp, too sharp
to handle life delicately,
my body too strong, too resolute
to be moved by anyone, too large,
too dangerous, too prone
to spearing or ramming those closest to me
with my horns.

I am a shark,
my teeth too sharp to kiss anyone
without tearing them to shreds,
my body too lean, too cold,
too slippery for anyone to hold,
my speed too rapid for anyone to grasp me
for long, my fight for freedom
the ultimate goal
of my life.

Tortoise

Eve stood, naked in the garden,
and closed her fist
around the last soft bit of fleshy ripe fruit,
squeezing the succulent pulp,
forcing the juice of knowledge between her fingers
to drip down her wrist and forearm
to the ground God walked upon –

so *this* was how it was going to be? Really?
An eternity for a few mere seconds
of simply wanting to know God better?
An eternity for simply aching
to see God more intimately?
An eternity for breaking
just one of God's rules,
put in place to keep her in her place,
set apart, from him?

The punishment was too extreme,
she knew this fully and well,
but hers was a jealous God, and she
was smaller and weaker and slower than he,
yet she would carry this new, separate Eternity
on her back forever, like a Tortoise
shouldering her world, hopeful.

And when Eternity runs out, finally,
she whispered through fruit-scented breath,
surely, surely, would he let me know him, then?

Wild Mushroom

deep in the dappled forest,
she broadened her billowy head –

poking up through the detritus of lost seasons,
her small self growing well and good
in the shadows of ancient trees –

she stretched up to meet the Sun
as full as she could reach,
> *(for she had learned reaching*
>> *from watching the trees),*

yet try as she might,
her whole self taut with her reaching,
her squat body remained, straining
to dislodge from her own tender roots
stuck firmly in the forest floor –

securing her deeply and eternally
to her toxic mushroom core

Sparkly

Her silver soul simmers
just beneath the shimmery
surface of her skin, radiating
heat, and sometimes when
she's laughing her deep blue laugh,
and dancing her sparkly dance,
her soul boils over, scalding
everyone within reach,
smelting her world
into an explosion
of sapphire
and light.

Eleanor

Eleanor had a peculiar habit
of working in her yard, watering flowers,
weeding the garden, mowing the grass,
in the middle of the afternoon,
in the hottest part of the day.

Eleanor enjoyed the sun's heat
baking her skin to a deep red tan,
like the clay in the southern corner
of her yard, but my, that sun was hot,
so Eleanor had developed

another peculiar habit,
of taking off her shirt
to do her mid-afternoon gardening –
her bare, full breasts brushing
against the zinnias

as she picked her tomatoes and cucumbers
in her garden, her sweat dripping down
her cleavage as she watered
her zucchini . . .
Eleanor simply sparkled

in the sun, happily
tending her flowers and vegetables,
her skin beautiful and glistening
as she pruned her plum trees,
her sweat-damp tendrils

of black hair escaping her
ponytail down her back,
and curling like baby garter snakes
against her long, inviting neck –
She herself was the centerpiece

of her garden, her masterfully
landscaped yard, singing away
in the sunshine, bare-breasted
under the sky –
Only, Eleanor lived in town.

Her habits were gracefully tolerated
for a few years, during her 20s,
her 30s, her 40s, and well on into
her 50s, even; people would gaze,
once, twice, maybe again, upon

her beauty, simply chuckle, and
force themselves, finally, to
look away – She was
in her own yard, after all,
on her own private property,

and there was nothing at all,
nothing at all, obscene
about the way Eleanor
looked or moved her body,
in fact, the townspeople

generally agreed, everything
about Eleanor was
just simply *delightful* –
she was, simply,
Eleanor,

pure in her nakedness,
innocent in her
naturalness, in fact,
most everyone had
enjoyed a mid-afternoon

conversation and a cold
glass of lemonade with
half-naked, happy Eleanor,
but eventually, something
happened –

Eleanor started sagging;
she developed a few
wrinkles, and
her skin started looking,
well, rather *odd*,

and Eleanor wasn't
tolerable anymore,
the townspeople agreed,
Eleanor wasn't
natural anymore,

they generally agreed, and
while Eleanor wasn't
quite *ugly*,
she was, they said,
rather *unbeautiful*,

so the sheriff, despite
his better judgment and
his own sagging chest,
finally made Eleanor
put her shirt back on.

Wanton

All winter and spring, we ached for summer
like a long-awaited lover, anticipated her charms
and voluptuous beauty, the cool depths of lake and shade –

and now, we were here again, staring out at the scenery
from our hot, sticky vinyl boat seats in the middle of the lake –
but her brown trees and bare limbs

of deep August shone out from the once-green Cookson hills
like a bleach-blonde's roots; her seductive fresh-water depths
and silky lake-cove curves of our memory

punctuated instead by this year's disappointment of the dry heat,
the chisel of too many days of record-breaking drought;
her shoreline showing

a white, dry line of rock – a ribbon around the lake
like her bra-strap peeking out from under her faded tank-top.
This summer, instead of the cool water

to dip our bodies into, or the deep green of our fantasy,
we see our summer romance for what she is –
[too fickle, too lean, too skeletal –]

we see for the first time our lover neglected . . .
struggling to maintain her beauty, shriveling up before our eyes
like a wanton woman,

undignified, squirming in her heat, in her lust.
So, embarrassed, we turn away in our boats,
dock them for another year,

and leave her
to her private shame.

Mother Nature

Mother Nature:
would she have used contraception?
Did she have a choice?
Did she want us? Did she plan for us?
5 Or were we the trap
with which she ensnared her lover's loyalty?
What makes her Mother?
Human mothers bake; feline mothers purr;
turtle mothers abandon their eggs in the sand.
10 Maybe we are wrong. Maybe it is not
a Mother we walk upon. Maybe it is only sand,
and she abandoned us long ago, like a turtle
with the weight of a world of consequences
as her shell.

15 Mother.
Mother.

Maybe she is not our Mother Earth, but
she has laid a trap to ensnare us, to lay up food
for her own true young . . . We are not her young.
20 We are not her future or her hope, but we
will nourish her true offspring.
We are her pantry, endlessly replenishing, so that
her children, worlds, histories, and fantasies,
need never hunger. They just cry,
25   "Mother, Mother. . ."
She turns on her oven, and nations disappear
to satisfy her true child's cravings;
she cracks lives apart over a spit-fire skillet
like cracking eggs, and she scrambles
30 our destinies for her children's breakfast.
She whisks our whirlwinds, our tragedies.

We feed her young.

our shadows into the sky

Shadows

We walked along the gravel road
closest to the lake at the campgrounds,
the four of us casting long shadows
across the rocky road in the night, the bats
barely missing our heads as they swooped down,
dipping into the shallows, our shadows
stretching across from here, to there, to the big dipper
peeking out through the tops of the sycamores,
all of us trying to race
our shadows into the sky.

Vacation

We came as shards of flint,
but we soaked our jagged edges
in the lake and the sun,
and we left as smooth as river stones,
changed enough
to skip across the choppy surface
of another school year

The Sweetest Incense

You flit among the sycamores
like the fresh April sunlight
glinting off the lake
in sparkling ripples,
5 washing the stillness
of another quiet winter away
like these gentle waves scrubbing
the river stones
into glimmering earth tones,
10 and you
are all angles and sunlight this year. *] ready for*

You are ready—
plunging head-first
into the brilliance
15 of another changing season,
as I lag behind you, wondering
when it was that you shucked off
your soft edges of babyhood –
knowing
20 that I must become ready
for another summer
to gently burn away
another year of your childhood,
smoldering it into the sweetest sacrifice,
25 a savory incense rising
from your beautiful life,
the purest wonder
under the sun.

There's always one kid like that

at the public pool
who wears orange goggles
missing the strap but
sucked down tight
on his face like *slook!*
bug eyes popping crazy
from the pressure

there's always one kid like that
who spends more time
under the water than on top,
swim trunks slipping down
his skinny, sun-browned frame,
head fully submerged
and butt-crack smiling at the world

there's always one kid like that
who sports a single flipper
because his sister stole the other one,
whose chlorine-slicked cowlicks
bob with each belly-laugh and belly-buster,

who spits and splashes
and blows pool-snot,
who sucks in big, deep breaths
before diving in again –
sucking up summer break
for all it's worth

Pre-K

You sat cross-legged on
the dirty Wal-Mart floor
as we waited in the long line
at the checkout, you
sucking your thumb and wearing
the shiny, satin, powder-blue new backpack
with the rainbow butterfly on it that
you picked out to take to your first
day of all-day pre-K;
my baby, so small,
too small to be out past ten p.m.
in a long line at an all-night supercenter,
too small to be forced to sit at
a hard wooden table at an all-day
pre-K classroom.

October Threads

strings of school buses,
the color of October,
golden fringe of youth

The Garage Sale

We were choking on the clutter,
shoved to the rafters in the attic, piled all pell-mell
in the corners and every spare inch of the garage, so jam-packed
we couldn't even park our cars in there anymore –

we were choking on too many clothes,
books, toys, dishes, movies – just too much stuff –
looking like a family of hoarders, navigating our way
through closets and cabinets congested
with junk piled on top of junk –

so we rose at four a.m. and hauled our clutter to the front yard
for a garage sale, because, we told ourselves,
people *had* garage sales –

I pulled your old stroller down from the attic,
its wheels unused for these last five years –
I knocked the cobwebs and dirt daubers' nests
off the handle and seat,
and opened it up again in the sunny air, cleaned and ready to roll
with a fresh, five-dollar price tag stuck on the top –

We hauled down the old crib you and your brother both used,
in pieces and missing one board, but still complete with memories
of lullabies and checking on you both
to make sure you hadn't stopped breathing in the night –

and I reminded myself to breathe now –
that we were having this garage sale,
that people did in fact, do this,
people had garage sales –

and we hauled down a mystery box from the attic,
packed away long ago with an assortment
of your size 18 month baby clothes:
a red and white frilly bathing suit,
sundresses with matching bloomers
in a green and yellow pineapple print –
ruffled short-sets with Strawberry Shortcake T-shirts –

46

and two pairs of pink baby sandals
[that stung my eyes with the sharpest image]
of your little sweet pudgy baby legs
sticking out from that stroller
as we walked around the block, the park, the zoo, the lake –
your baby-fine hair in pigtails
sticking straight out from the tippy-top of your head
under two powder-pink bows – your sweet baby-girl face smiling
around your chapped, chubby thumb stuck firmly in your mouth –

and when I came to, in the middle of our garage sale,
I saw your big-girl hand shove a five-dollar bill
down into the pocket of your skinny, big-girl jeans,

and I watched, helpless,
as your stroller was carried away by strangers
down the road in the back of some evil, red pick-up truck –

I tried to breathe –
my eyes stinging like hell under my dark sunglasses,
but I choked up again on all our clutter,
remembering with a vengeance
why I hated the guts out of garage sales.

waiting

it gets harder and harder to wait,
but then the waiting becomes comfortable
and it's the doing that becomes
too tiresome, too hard
to believe in

the bad part about
all this waiting is
that you've grown up
in the meantime
and all my "we'll do it later,"
and all my "we have to wait
until the money comes in,"
or all my "I'm sorry, son,
but it just didn't work out
this time," like every time,
I think and you think, but
you've waited long enough
to know, you've waited
long enough to understand

that the waiting is what
we have done and will do
because that is all we ever do,
so you don't say
anything,
but you quit believing
in anything
anymore

A Wild Place

Along the rocky shore
is a wild place
under the mangle
of locust trees
and slender sycamore stalks,
where black bear
come down to drink,
and brown-skinned boys
reel in the years
on brittle line.

Belly of the Whale

It's the belly of August,
and we've spent all our money
on school supplies
and school clothes
and electricity
to beat the heat,

but it could be worse,
I remind myself
as I pass
a weathered,
paint-peeling,
wood-frame house

with all the windows open,
weeds grown up to the eaves,
and twenty cloth diapers
strung out on a line –
oh yes,
it could be worse.

Scraps

She's hungry
for the flock of birds
overhead
like flecks of pepper
in a big bowl
of blue sky soup . . .

but she drives on . . .

She's thirsty
for October trees
overflowing
with rich wet colors
and the liquid light
of tree glow, pasture walks,
and front-yard football . . .

but she drives on . . .

pushing through her daily duties
and leftover scraps of a mother's guilt.

The Apology

What was I supposed to have done?
Apologize for the piles of laundry,
the stacks of bills, the unwashed dishes,
the toys strewn all over the yard like so much garbage,
the bedrooms so messy we carved a path
through the clothes and trash from door to bed
just so we wouldn't trip in the night
if you called out to us in the darkness –

was I supposed to tell you I'm sorry
for the hours of homework you had to endure every night,
or the nights I had to work so long that I had no time or energy
left over for you?

What was I supposed to say
when we could not be there at your school parties
or ballgames or concerts, when no kids slept over,
or asked you to sleep over, how could I apologize
for you still scared of the dark, for dreading school every day,
for feeling so lonely and angry?

Was it my fault?
Is it my fault?
How could I have stopped
any of this?
How can I change our past
when it is gone?

I'm sorry, so very, very sorry,
        but I still don't know –
            I never knew –
                what to do –

        I don't know how
        to fix this.

The Chair

She had started disappearing again. It
began gradually like it always did, with
her hands; her work was taken for
granted because no one could see
her hands doing the work, and then
it was her feet that disappeared next,
though they didn't really disappear, rather
they just blended into the ground she
walked upon, camouflaging her legs
and lower torso until she became
just another bit of furniture in
the cluttered house, like the
lamp, plugged into the wall, or
the armoire, too heavy to move. She
looked out, one last time before
her eyes disappeared, to see
all of herself gone now, except
her handless arms, catching
her family like a sturdy, well-worn
armchair, always open, always
comforting, and her silky, long
hair, perfumed and covering her
squirming children like a favorite
blanket, slowly becoming thread-bare
with age and use, completely unable
to shelter anyone from this great,
encroaching Invisible.

Sunshine Children

sunshine children on a sacred Saturday:
tea-towel capes and front-yard football –
let them fly; let them play.

silver kitchen spoons, dirt-encrusted, lay
beside rivers carved by hands so small:
sunshine children on a sacred Saturday.

sweet shrieks of joy from the chill water-hose spray –
a slick front porch and harmless falls –
let them fly; let them play.

muddy-kneed blue jeans, patched and faded, fray
from another back-yard bear-hunt crawl:
sunshine children on a sacred Saturday.

their innocent laughter rode the warm sunrays:
"Come play with me! Come play!" they called –
but we let them fly; we let them play,

and now despite the wistful dreams we pray,
childhood never stays; it never stalls –
sunshine children on a sacred Saturday –
we let them fly; we let them play.

Soaking

They're good kids, really,
out on the trampoline,
bare-footed,
with a rolled-up sleeping bag,
throwing it back and forth
at each other,
watching it bounce
as they jump,
out in the golden sunshine
of a late October afternoon,
soaking up the last few hours
of Autumn warmth
before the cold snap
runs them inside.

A Boy's Garden

his small, dirty hands,
busy planting marigolds,
patted down the earth,
while his three-year-old bare feet
trampled rows of okra seed

The Best Gift

my proud son brings me
a sunny dandelion,
a reverent gift

Little Poinsettias in the Snow

in memory of the precious children of Newtown, Connecticut
December 14, 2012

Little poinsettias in the snow,
> *like the ones the children*
> *had cut out of construction paper*
> *just the day before,*
> *with their small hands*
> *trying to cut along the lines,*
> *and hung so proudly on display*
> *in the school hallway,*

bright red leaves, belonging not to this environment,
strewn across the frozen world
> *like a million drops of blood,*
> *an irremovable stain*
> *of the slaughter of lives,*
> *the massacre of innocents,*

cruelly plucked from their stems,
ripped from the safety of the greenhouse, wilting instantly
upon contact with the inexplicable cold,

breaking the gardener's heart who stands by, helpless,
with no remedy for this pain,
> *like the parents, broken by injuries*
> *no bandages or kisses can heal,*
> *shattered by an evil no prayer can dispel,*
> *for their grief is too much to bear,*
> *their ice is too thick to melt,*

still we kneel in this blizzard, and we pray for those we have left:
> *Oh God. Watch over these children.*
> *Please, God, watch over your babes.*
> *Keep them safe, and keep them healthy.*
> *Keep them happy and strong and secure.*

And we cherish and we remember.
Wailing, we gather the wilted leaves.

Wine-dark Bath

They were singing "Itsy Bitsy Spider"
to scare away the dark night
they were driving through,
trying to calm themselves
from the storm raging around them,
when they skidded on the wet highway,
hydroplaning the car –
rolling, rolling, over and over again
until it landed, upside down,
in the flooded, rushing creek –
She was instantly knocked unconscious
when the car crashed to a stop,
and her children in the backseat
quit singing, stunned into silence
by their whiplash bruises
across their little chests and necks –

they sat waiting and whispering
for Momma to wake up,
to help them
unbuckle their seat belts . . .
            hurry, Momma, hurry,
to help them crawl out
of their crooked booster seats
in the upside down car –
to tell them that everything
would be ok, to tell them
to keep on singing,
that they would be home soon,
safe out of the rain,
safe from the thunder –

but then another crash came,
and the water rushed in
like a wine-dark bath,
and no one
ever sang
again.

Worn

My father's worn Bible
is stapled together at the seams
where the leather cover
has pulled apart from use.
He holds his Bible gingerly,
like a difficult prayer,
and I wonder if he's found
what he's been looking for.

Apothecary

Propped against the well-worn barstool at the counter,
the sweet, old pharmacist rests his arthritic knees,
and tries to rub away the ache in his knuckles.
He grits his teeth against the pain,
the lines in his forehead testament
to his years in the profession.

He peers over his bifocals
to count out the life-saving pills.
He believes in the power of pills,
the importance of life, the grace of God.
His starched, white smock hides the scars
of his recent quadruple bypass surgery, as he stands here,
day after day, doling out these pills, mixing these elixirs,
caring for his neighbors.

They know him as his family knows him –
the kind pharmacist who will leave his own bed
in the middle of the night to open the shop and
fill a prescription for a sick child recently released
from the emergency room, who gives the good medicine away
when the families cannot pay for it, who goes in early
when his mind is fresh to measure and re-measure
the life-saving mixture
for a premature infant . . .

He understands there is no room for error.
He, like the medicine, is a part of their lives.

He is well past retirement age,
but he wipes the sweat from his forehead;
cleans the smudges off his glasses,
rubs his arthritic knees and knuckles,
and counts out his pills,
each one a precious second of life,
meant to be swallowed whole,
and digested slowly.

Bottom-feeders

In August that year, we were so poor, I either
went barefoot or wore my sister's old sandals –
so I went barefoot on the hot asphalt, crossing
the road to and from work at the soda shop
where Mr. Burton let me borrow a pair
of his good dress shoes to work at the counter,
wiping up and pulling the pop, sweeping
the crickets and the junebugs from the corners,
saving them in a big coffee can he gave me,
saving up those bugs
for when I got to go fishing with you . . .
      me and Mr. Burton filled up that coffee can
      in no time, Dad, no time . . .
then I'd take his good shoes off, and leave them
under his desk for the next day; he'd close up shop,
and I'd cross back over that hot blacktop road
on my way home –
my asphalt-blistered soles stinging with each step,
my smile, gap-toothed and poor, sucking in
the free, end-of-the-day, super-syrupy cherry limeade
Mr. Burton always sent home with me –
me knowing full well that's why
I had to have my last tooth pulled –
      Dad, what boy at 12 has to pay for his own
      dental care?
but I sucked down that cold pop all the same . . .
the cherries so shiny and red, like fishin' bobbers,
the soda water so refreshing . . . so like the lake water
in that shiny picture of you out fishing
with your girlfriend's kids – Remember, Dad,
that day you said you'd take me to that fishing spot
where the biggest bass you ever saw flew
on top of that lake water, shiny, chomping
at the gnats buzzing the surface?
You told me fish were like people –
some people danced on top of the water,
and some people sank in the mud
like no-good bottom-feeders.

61

I remember.

I had to pay to have my tooth pulled,
but I saved just enough money
to buy a shiny, new, red tackle-box,
three new bobbers, and some hooks
to tie onto my old cane pole . . .
I stayed up all night tying and retying
those new hooks to the bobbers,
but the next morning,
you left without me . . .
and you left without that shiny picture
of you fishing with your girlfriend's kids.

I remember, Dad,
later that same day, I put that picture in my pocket,
and I walked across the hot asphalt to work.
Mr. Burton saw me coming, he said,
and he felt like going fishing. He closed the shop,
in the middle of the day, and he fixed us both
a big, cold, cherry limeade. We sucked it down,
all of it, as we crossed the blacktop road,
walked straight out of town, four miles,
down to his farm pond.

We fished for bottom-feeders that day.
I sank my asphalt-blistered soles
down into the cool mud and ripped
your shiny picture to shreds,
the fragments dancing on the surface
of Mr. Burton's murky pond, for only a minute,
before sinking in the mud,
sure to be sucked up
by those no-good, bottom-feeders.

Rock bottom

One day I thought,
    "This is it.
        I've finally hit rock bottom,"
but I was wrong,
and a big wave came,
washed away that layer of rock,
and left behind a sinking, sticky sand.

I thought,
    "Now, this is it.
        There's no place left for me to go,"
but I was wrong,
and a big wave came,
washed away that layer of sand,
and left behind a big, black hole.

I fell through the expanse,
completely alone,
but strangely calm,
because nothing,

Nothing

could hurt me now,
except the big, dark empty.

Drummer Boy

When I was five, Daddy,
you smelled like wood-smoke and safety,
as I laid my head against your chest,
your heart softly pulsing my life's rhythm –
your life-beat my lullaby –
my small fingers tapping out time
to the rhythm of your heart . . .

and when I was too big for you to hold,
too old to lay my head against your chest,
I still tapped out time with your pulse,
even when you weren't looking,
pounding on pots and pans in the kitchen
with Mama's wooden spoons,
hollering to you through the walls
of our falling-down rent house,
out to where you stood in the back yard –
you trying to fix our broken-down lawn mower –
and me shouting, "Daddy, hey, Daddy,
can you hear me?"
and pounding louder, ever louder
to make sure you heard . . .

and later,
when I was too old to pound on pots and pans,
I hammered nails with you,
building together the beautiful walls
of our first real home –
my twelve-year-old hands gripping the hammer,
pounding the nails into the walls
of my soon-to-be bedroom,
so proud –
so proud –
my hammer keeping rhythm with your hammer,
as I hollered to you through the unfinished door frame
of my new room,
"Daddy, can you hear me?"

And when the money ran out,
and we had to sell our home we built together –

when you left us all standing
there in that broken-down rent house, begging
you to stay –   *please, just stay* –
I pounded my fists to a pulp,
busting holes through the flimsy walls
of that damn rent house—
bloodying my knuckles—
wailing over the rhythm of my pain –
"Daddy! Hey, Daddy! Can you hear me?"

. . . and three years later,
when you still had not heard me,
I bought a used drum set with the money
I earned that summer mowing yards
with that same piece-of-shit mower
you left behind,
and I beat those drums to a pulp
in that rent house garage –
I beat them loud and wild –
hoping that just maybe, *this time*, you'd hear me –

and years, oh so many years later,
when I pounded the nails into the walls
of my dream home with my son and my grandson,
I hammered loud, so loud . . .

. . . and I bought another drum set just this year –
brand-new; I play it every day,
the old hippy that I am, now in my sixties,
and you long since gone from my life,
your heartbeat long since mute,
but I play wild, and I play loud,
and I still beat out the pulse of your life –
I tap out the time with my whole being –
because Daddy, Daddy,
I want to make you hear me.

Ohio

you left us
for the cold winters
of Ohio.

you took that job
and you left us
for the unknown

because the unknown
must have been better
than muddling

through our hell
here, in this
humid state

of passions
and obstinance –
you left us –

we, hiding in our
poverty like
fiddlebacks in the attic,

clamping down hard
on our roots like
coyotes on a bone –

you left us.

Betrayal

is a hard sport;
it first requires you
to give up on yourself, and then,
once you have lost yourself,
losing others is easy.

The Fight

She'd been bullied too often by Life,
that hateful bitch, and consequently,
she'd developed an unhealthy dependency on Sleep.
Life had knocked the shit out of her, held her down,
and run off with all the people she loved the most
until she was left completely alone,
that is, alone except for Sleep . . .

she'd thought of running off with Death,
but Death was too complicated and possessive of a lover –
she didn't have the energy to feed his passion, and besides,
Sleep was so much easier to fall in with;
he was gentle, steady and predictable,
and for years, she never even had to try to make him come to her;
he was always, simply, *there*, that is, until lately,
when Sleep had taken to bouts of crankiness,
whining incessantly that she'd taken him for granted,
making her feel *uncomfortable*,
and only staying with her an hour here
or two hours there each night,
leaving her to panic, worried
that Life would come looking for her
before she could be safe with Sleep again . . .

and then one night, Sleep didn't come at all . . .
and he stayed gone the next night, and the next,
until finally, she figured out that he'd left her for good.
She opened her eyes, and sure enough,
she saw that slut whore Life sneaking up on her –
flirting with the sunrays breaking through her windows –
and she knew then that she had a fight on her hands.
So, she mustered all her courage, went out the door,
and faced her greatest enemy,
yelling loud enough to raise the dead:
        "Come on, bitch, let's get this over with!"

Magic

The sweet gum tree
was the only green left
in the drought-brown neighborhood,

pulling water into her trunk
from her prolific roots, her offspring
shooting up all around her,

sheltered by her shade and her magic
of finding moisture enough
to sustain them all.

Kites

Today was laundry day,
and so I folded my
freshly laundered panties, only
they looked like my mother's,

5 stretched across the rear,
and as white and thin as
cotton can get.
Holding them,

thinking about laundry
10 and growing up
in my old home,
I chuckled.

Kites, my brother
and I called them,
15 and we'd laugh as
we stretched

and pulled them
between us, or
put them over
20 our heads for

a mask, the clean,
fresh scent of
dryer sheet filling
our nostrils,

25 and so I hold
my kite now,
proud to finally
fit into

my mother's britches.

My Mother's Hand

My mother's cool hand swept
the wisps of hair from my forehead, and soothed
my childhood dreams as I lay protected
in her lap, in her arms, inhaling
5 the perfume of her wrist.

My mother's firm hand kept
me steady on my bicycle, and rinsed
the blood from my knee when
she could not keep me from falling,
10 her cool breath more soothing than salve.

My mother's warm hand held
my head to her heart as I wept, and turned
my tears to wisdom as
she counted my blessings for me,
15 her calm voice easing my sorrow.

My mother's brave hand led
me safely through the wild winds blowing,
and covered me with shelter, till I
was strong enough
20 to stand the winds alone.

My mother's gentle hand
slipped softly from my own,
and I opened my arms
to find her there.

Legacy

my blood—

> Although you were cut from my body
> upon the moment of your birth,

your blood—

> your cry branded your life's imprint
> upon my heart, searing forever

my blood—

> our connection as mother and daughter
> with an irremovable mark,

your blood—

> the mark of

my blood as your blood—

> my mother's legacy.

she dreamed of running

She dreamed of running

past her Parkinson's, past
her wheelchair and her walker, past
the dying people lined up
in the nursing home hallway, and right on out
the heavy glass doors –

she dreamed of running

past the nightmares of her widowhood, past
the grief of single-motherhood, past
the graves of her sisters, her nephews, her
brother, her mother, her father, past
the wild elms waving their farewells, down
the old dirt road, and right on out
into the open pasture, riddled
with Indian paintbrush and black-eyed Susan, past
the cow pond and the fishing shed, out
to where the cotton patch of her childhood met
the clear November sky –

she dreamed of running

down along the river,

it's hard to tell
the sound of wind
rushing through leaves
from the sound of current
rushing over stone,
or the quick snap of a campfire
from footsteps cracking fallen sticks
along the bank —

down along the river,
sometimes laughter
fades into birdcalls
and the fog of one's memory
fades into the mist
just above the rippling water
flowing forever onward,
dancing gently
below the clouds

The Birds

Crazed out of her mind with the high fever and the infection the doctors couldn't treat because she was allergic to all the antibiotics that they tried, she stayed in intensive care at the Arkansas Memorial Hospital through Christmas, crying out for a smoke, angry with the nurses, accusing them of stealing her cigarettes, for being cruel and smoking them right there in front of her in her hospital room, and then when she pointed crazy at the bright red poinsettias on the shelf in her room, and screamed at us to get those black birds out of her room! when she kept telling us over and over in frenzied tones, eyes wild with fear, about how those blackbirds flew round in a circle above her bed and how they all fell dead one by one around her, we were convinced she had to be out of her mind, but then, three days later, when her fever broke, and all those blackbirds in Arkansas fell dead out of the sky, and no one really had any good explanation for it, well, then we weren't so sure, and we thought, maybe, just maybe, she hadn't really been out of her mind at all, but instead, perhaps, those blackbirds had been in hers.

Alone

For a while today, I was lonely on a sunny Sunday afternoon, but then it occurred to me that I really didn't know what it meant to be lonely, for you, Grandmother, were spending another night alone in the hospital, another night alone in your fear, in your insecurity, facing your impending death, alone.

You, Grandmother, knew what it meant to really be alone when you were younger than I am now; your husband dead before your 35th birthday, and you alone in the waiting room of the hospital to hear the news from his doctor that he didn't make it through the surgery,

and when your children all finally left your nest, you were left alone with no one to help you shoulder the grief, the emptiness, no one to hold you when you wept, no one to grab you when you fell apart, no one to help you get home when you drove, lost, in the darkness, trying to find your way back to where you last were not alone.

You went days without visitors, in the dead cold winters; you went weeks without phone calls in the summers when your kids and grandkids were gone to camps, to vacations, without you, without a thought of you, and you went months without repairs or requests being answered . . . because you couldn't stand to be a burden . . .

yet now, you, scared, small, feeble in a hospital bed, you no longer prefer being lonely to being a burden . . . but no one comes for you now. You face this darkness alone, and your loneliness in the middle of this sunny Sunday afternoon makes a mockery of mine.

Little by little,

worn down to nothing
but a soft bundle
in a temporary bed
in a temporary room

filled with buzzing, beeps
and a constant *whoosh whoosh* –
a steady stream of daily nurses and aides,
doctors twice a day, the snack cart,
the lunch cart, the dinner cart,
someone to open the shades,
someone to close the shades,
someone to prop up the pillows,
someone to remove them,
always someone for some thing,

and little by little,
breath by breath, and drip by drip,
she sank away
into crumbs in her comforter
and bits of bruises in her memory –

waiting

for someone

What a widow carries with her

are mulberries and mimosas,
yellow bikinis in a kitchen drawer,
outgrown by daughters
and granddaughters long ago—
empty hog pens and cattle runs,
barns where the tack lay unused,
troughs and lots devoid of horses,
garden plots gone back to pasture.

What a widow carries with her
are rusty slides and slip-shod teeter-totters,
too-silent swings and martin houses
with loose boards — her own shingles
flying off her roof with each passing storm—
bird nests in her chimney
and lizards in her den, cracks in her hands
from loading in logs to feed her wood-stove
in wind-chilled winters.

What a widow carries with her
are calico cats gone missing
and border collies long buried,
coffee gone cold in her pot,
a cast iron skillet rusting on a quiet stove—
memories of trains and doors—
spirits too heavy for her purse—
and flavors so bland that no amount of salt
can bring back the taste.

What a widow carries with her
are leftover smoke and ashtrays
from cigarettes rolled long ago at her table,
burn marks glittering like stars
across cedar-scented quilts
that she still carries
gently, so very, very gently,
to lay across the bed
she once shared.

Spare Ashes

We knew it was the last day you would ever be home, where the
lingering smells of butterscotch, smoke, whiskey and catfish still
slipped off the wood-paneled walls into our memories of nights
spent here around your scarred kitchen table, playing pitch and
moon, sharing cold cathead biscuits and salty tomatoes, the kids
in the den sleeping deep in ratty old quilts in front of the fireplace,
safe from those howling coyotes in the night.

We knew it was the last time we'd walk in and see you sitting
there in your chair at the kitchen table, smoking your cigarettes,
flicking your ashes everywhere, and reaching for that grimy old
salt shaker to salt up those fries you shouldn't have been eating
with that chili cheese coney you shouldn't have been eating,
either.

We knew when we heated up your coffee and watched your life
swirl in ours like the cream in your cup, that this would be your
last cup to ever go cold; we inhaled the aroma and watched you
miss your mouth . . . the stickers in our memory pricking us like
barefoot children in the pasture, the coyotes' howls carrying you
further and further away.

We knew it was the last pot of tea we'd boil in the metal pan
on your propane stove, and we knew when we carried in those
rotting logs that we were building our last fire up high in your
fireplace; we drank all the wine you had left in your cabinets,
watching the fire dance itself down to its last embers, knowing
in our guts that when those last sparks shot up into the night, that
this time we'd finally have to clear out all these ashes for good.

Still, when all was cleared and polished, the coffee cups rinsed,
the salt shakers from every room collected and set like sentries on
your table, we couldn't help but keep the kitchen light on for you,
just the way you always liked it; we couldn't help but crack the
window by your empty bed, just the way you always used to –
so you could breathe at night, you said –

only now we left it open in case your spirit crept back in, weary
from crying us to sleep on the coyotes' songs, searching for salt,
whispering through creaking walls, and sending spare ashes
dancing through empty rooms.

The Grace of Monarchs

orange petal wings
welcome October home as
monarchs grace the woods

Homesick

She didn't want to go, but she had to.
She didn't want to go on this journey, far away
from her children, her sister, her husband,
but she could not stay. She had to go.

Kicking and screaming, angry at the inevitability
of her passage, she died. She left –
would never return to us in this form;
her entire life packed into this small, bronze urn.

We drank our communion to her, in our own way,
the rich red wine and smooth dark chocolate,
mixed with our laughter and our grief,
already full of a homesickness we could not shake.

Cherry Blossom

This snapshot of my grandfather in his 20s, handsome
in his WWII Army fatigues, smiling brilliantly
from the undisturbed temple steps in Japan,
under the only cherry tree in bloom, the only cherry tree
left standing in the post-bomb, charred landscape –
it's this snapshot of my grandfather,
standing there so handsomely,
holding hands with a beautiful Japanese woman,
that makes my mother wonder
if she has any more sisters,
and makes my grandmother curse
over the cigarette in her teeth.

Dry

Mosquitos and Love:
both bite the fire out of you
and suck you dry

George

He was just another old man in a café,
propped up on a cane, befriending
strangers in a frenzy;

it was no matter
5 who he was, or who he had been –
no matter

he had flown fighter planes, flown the circus, flown
two wives through two lives . . .
no matter now. . .

10 he was just another old man in a café,
propped up on a cane, waiting
for someone to pick up

his last check.

Black Rain

in memory of the "other WWII casualties" of Hiroshima and Nagasaki

their fields and paddies stretched
before the ruins of their village, black and dry,
seared by the merciless bomb;

the survivors cowered in the shadows,
their burned lungs struggling for breath, their parched tongues
lapping at whatever hint of moisture they could find;

their lives in ashes, they prayed for deliverance
and wept for salvation, so when the first drops fell,
mothers lifted their children high to the blessed rain,

grandfathers opened their mouths wide to the heavens,
everyone danced in the ruins, singing
and drinking in the promise of renewal—

only too late did they realize the rain was black,
and the bomb massacred them a second time
as they drank their death,

confused
and crying out
for mercy—

Breath

mildew laden air
chokes my lungs with each pained breath;
starving fish float here.
I rush past the stagnant pond –
gasping – to remember life

Resolve

broken clouds resolve
to search for the sun's respite,
damming their tired rain

Lost Harvest

the earth cracked under his boots
like his hands, split and bleeding from plowing,
like his feet, bruised from digging his heels into his homestead,
like his faith, brittle from pleading for rain,
hoping for something to grow besides dust

his eyes stung with the sharp debris of hope
as he scanned the horizon,
trying to will the fair-weather clouds
into sustaining thunderheads
by the intensity of his concentration,
by the depth of his sheer need

the sun sneered back at him;
her heat rose from the earth in waves
where the corn should have been,
scorched his will, and dried up his future
like his last seeds, her angry breath
driving them away in dust devils
across the fallow topsoil
of his drought-ridden dreams.

his life fell into the cracked, parched soil
of his destiny, his young wife, shriveled and grey
as the dust coating the lean-to, his children, buried
before breathing their first words,
the moisture of life seared out of them
by this hell of dust and windblown dry
cracked and bleeding desolate air
of his lost harvest

Visiting

Slack-jawed from the stroke that finally paralyzed your body
like your absence paralyzed our family for years,
drool crusted in the corners of your mouth,
like a scab crusting over a fresh wound,
your ashen lips, dry and cracked, inking old blood
onto your crisp, white, hospital pillow,

we filed in, one by one, to try to settle what we could with you,
all of us finally collected, writing our own fictions of your life,
feigning concern, feigning a tenderness
that we all wished had been but never was, feigning a forgiveness
for what you should have been:
> grandfather, father, husband, uncle, brother,
feigning a memory that we had been something, *someone* to you –

imagining that we had shared something more with you
than just this stale air settling like dust
over your last few minutes of life, we, gathered here, together,
collectively acknowledging your existence as if to prove our own,
granting you nothing more, really,
than what we'd grant any old, pathetic stranger.

The Stand

His family grew up tall
and strong around him, like
a stand of wild sycamores,
rooted in the rocks of
his years of hard work,
sprung from the seeds of
his softly spoken prayers.

Black Dutch

*Many Choctaw great-grandparents, as well as many other
American Indians, claimed they were "Black Dutch" to avoid
persecution and forced assimilation*

What would I do, if they came to take you from me?
To take you from my arms, to unwrap you
from my blankets, to unsing you
from my lullabies, to unpray you
from my prayers?

What would I do, if they came to take you from me?
To take you from my fire, to warm you instead
with their stories in their language, with their heroes' legends,
filling your mind with their promises, your belly with their food,
growing you like an orchid under their metered daily waterings,
[doling out compassion with their civilized threats of hell,]
with their promises of their heaven, if only you'd believe,
if only you'd concede that your parents were savages,
that you wanted the True Light?

What should I have done, my daughter, my son, to keep you
from bleeding as I bled? To keep you
from dying as I died – to keep you
from being driven in herds without mercy?

Becoming Black Dutch was easy.

Fox

On the day you disappeared,
the fox turned up dead in the field,
already covered with flies;

the buck appeared in broad daylight,
stirred by the confusion in the air;

the biggest, greenest snake doctor I'd ever seen
rammed hard into the kitchen window,
and the hawks circled our house for hours.

I felt the weight of your absence settle,
heavy as the air carrying the pungent smell of carrion,

and I watched the children gather with their sticks
to poke what was left

of that fox.

Picnic

I always thought it was a table,
the crumbling brick grave house
topped with a concrete slab,
out in the pasture between the two elms,
5 ringed round by cream-colored irises
and a well-worn coyote path.

It looked like a table to me,
and it might as well have been,
for all the times my cousins and grandma
10 and I trekked out to it with sacks
of bread and honey sandwiches
and bologna and crackers.

We picnicked on the grave house slab
and left our crumbs behind
15 so many summer days, that now I wonder
if the young Creek Indian man buried there
liked bologna and crackers; I wonder
if his spirit came out to fly with us
on those warm summer afternoons
20 as we all nourished our souls together
among the irises in the pasture,
breathing in the daylight
sweetened by honey
and bread.

Maggie

Maggie stared long and deep,
straight down the sightline from her well,
to the little graves beneath the two old elms.

She'd planted the irises there
5 because she knew they were good medicine,
and even though her medicine

hadn't been strong enough
to cure her sweet twins from the whooping cough
that killed them in the deep of last winter,

10 she knew that these irises,
the exact color of her babies' first teeth,
were still good medicine for her own pain

that hit her hard in the stomach
and behind her teeth.
15 She tended these cream-colored irises

like a fervent new mother,
still nursing a newborn sorrow,
protecting her children from the living.

Cream-colored iris,

the color of teeth and bone,
sorrow's vicious bite

Coyote

Maggie pointed with her lips to the new brick grave house with the concrete slab out in the pasture beneath the two elms, next to the flat sandstone marking her twin babies' graves.

It was a sturdy grave house, paid for with the white man's
5 government check she had received for her son's service in WWII, and what was left of his shattered body, a meager bundle of bones that she could not even hold in her arms.

"He's there," she told the young Army private freshly home from the war who'd come to pay his respects.

10 "Thank you, ma'am," he said softly to her, his hat in his fists, his eyes on the ground in front of them.

Maggie only nodded and went back to drawing water from her well as the young soldier went out to her son's grave. She took a long drink of cool water to wash the new grief out of her throat
15 that came up on her when the soldier had driven up her driveway to ask about her son.

They'd been brothers in the war, he told her, respectfully not looking her in the eye, and he was sorry for her loss, he said, and he wanted her to know that her son had been a good man, that he
20 had been a brave man.

She watched the young soldier kneel down at her son's spirit house and place a pouch of tobacco by his headstone. She turned away when she saw the man's shoulders shake with his sobs and went back into her house, leaving the man to grieve her son alone.

25 She didn't know when he finally left. She never heard his car door open or shut, or hear him drive away down the road, but she knew he would be back again. She knew it as sure as her son's spirit still whispered through the elm leaves mingling with the sunlight of her twin babies' souls, because the pouch of tobacco was gone,
30 and the coyotes had worn a fresh path around the grave.

The Tree

The single sycamore tree in the front lawn had always been
a pleasant afterthought, its strength ever-ready to be
admired by the homeowners and passers-by
when it was convenient, when it was comfortable
for them to take a quick break from their all-important
lives to notice its beautiful, lingering presence.
But this year, the sycamore leaves fell too soon. The tree
groaned in July, and it could not wait any longer
for anyone to notice. It was most inconvenient, really.

Had the rain only come like it was supposed to, had
the tree only waited like it was expected to, had
the leaves only held on and grown to the size of
dinner plates that turned golden in mid-October, then
all would have been well, the homeowners
delighted, even, would have been pleasantly
amused, perhaps, to clean the mess in the coolness
of the Autumn afternoons, wielding their rakes
like dancers – how very pleasant indeed, how
very convenient, that would have been.

But no, the tiny, stunted leaves would not
hold on until October. They turned brown and
fell and fell and fell. They demanded too
much attention, made too big a mess. It was
most uncomfortable, most inconvenient, indeed,
for these pretty homeowners to be expected
to pick up all the scatterings in the scorching
sun, sweating unpleasantly and profusely,
just because the tree couldn't keep itself together.

It was most unpleasant and unbecoming, really,
that this once-brilliant tree would not simply *wait*,
as everyone wanted it to wait,
for a more convenient, cooler season,
to go about its quiet business
of dying.

October Trees

Last night,
the October trees
turned golden
in the crescent moonlight
and shone out
from the Autumn sunrise,
bright as day.

Golden

golden pecan leaves
scatter across the red sand-
stone of dry creek beds

Oklahoma

Oklahoma, I love you.
These trees of Southern California are beautiful,
but they are not my trees.
These palms and smooth, pale barks slip
through my hands, but they are not
the black walnut, the pecan, the oak that
I can rub my hands raw against the roughness
of changing seasons, their acorns cutting into
my bare feet, their fallen leaves changing slowly
from the pressures of ten thousand years into
the oil coursing through the blood-red soil, deep
inside my earth.

For All She's Worth

Oklahoma whispers your name in the night,
and in your dreams, you turn to her,
wrap your arms around her,
and take her for all she's worth.

Tender of Flesh

Their machines are bigger than us, and they push harder
than our tender bodies know how to push – we who are
but flesh and blood, ground into the earth by their brute force,
their artificial strength mocking the strength we carry
in our words and our mere hands – we who are
organic, like the sands of the Canadian River bed, a mighty river,
yet unable to defend itself against the industrial progress
of workers arriving in droves like a legion of demons,
glittering like money in their lines of RVs,
spinning promises like the Pied Piper, exploiting our years
of poverty and desperation, buying our loyalty, our land,
our water, our children's years.

When we first heard they were coming,
we tried to speak for the River, who could not speak
for itself. We said to the workers, please,
don't come through here. We said,
you must be men and women of reason. We said, please,
listen to us.

But they would not listen. They could not hear
over their machines. So we spoke louder;
we shouted over their clamor. We said,
sometimes life is more important than money. We said,
don't take advantage of us because we are poor,
don't roll right over us because you can,
because we aren't made of steel and fuel. We said, please,
don't patronize our desperation with your economic double-talk,
please, please, please –

But they answered with their machines, rolling over all of us,
human and river, blood and clay,
grinding us deeper into the battered earth, reminding us
that steel is bigger than flesh, that industry is mightier than earth,
that they are stronger than a simple drop of water,
that they are the winners in the courts, the holders of the law –

And we who wish only to protect our rivers,
our earth, our way of life – we who are
pushed aside by brute force because we who are

weaker than steel – we are the losers to these machines
fueled by immense greed for more jobs for more masses, more
manufacturing for more money, more transporting for more
tar sands and poison across the countryside,
through our ancient aquifers, shattering the very ground
our children run and laugh and grow on – we can do Nothing,
but cry out for awareness – we can do Nothing,
but chain our tender flesh to cold steel – we can do Nothing,
but warn our children what lies beneath the surface –
what demons of efficiency course through the clay
beneath the seemingly innocent pastures of plenty.

And we who are
but flesh and blood – we who are
but water and clay – we who are
strong in spirit but tender of flesh – we can do Nothing,
but teach our children to listen.

This

Seventy-two degrees with a full moon rising slowly
on a pink horizon, and an orange Oklahoma sun sparkling
across the rippling farm pond: It's evenings like these – listening

to the cicadas and frogs singing, my ten-year-old son zinging
shots out of his pellet gun, watching
my dad and daughter feeding the catfish, guzzling
wine with my mother and laughing
about the family gossip –

It's evenings like these –
the air soft on our temples,
our lives scented with the smell
of freshly mown hay –

that I know *this* is why
I stay in this state for less pay than I'm worth,
this is why
we all choose Oklahoma in the end –

Oklahoma red is in our blood,
and we feel her seasons, like the weather,
changing in our veins.

Summer Congregation

Snake doctors zoom in –
a summer congregation,
buzzing by the pond.

Sucker

What a million dollars is to me,
I am to a tick:

a little bite here,
a little bite there,

and the tick could feed itself for years
off my iron-poor blood.

Heat

The heat is almost as oppressive as my paycheck,
almost as offensive as the IRS,
almost as hateful as my tax bill,
almost as heavy as my life.

If I pass out for a few days,
I wonder if the heat
will burn up everything I owe,
burn off all my debts

like it burned off the green from the grass,
the leaves off the trees,
the fun out of summer—
burn off my duties and responsibilities

without completely obliterating me?

Event after WoodyFest

Two a.m. in Oklahoma July,
and the thirty-two-year-old drunk bachelor
lifts the edge of the chain link fence,
crawls under, strips naked, and dives
into the closed, dark, and silent
public pool.

He floats on his back,
his genitals covered slightly
by the moonshine on the water,
biceps rippling beautifully
with each backstroke—
trespassing for his baptism.

His friends and family's accusations
of "Why aren't you married yet?"
fall off his body like these soft drops
of municipal chlorine, gliding across
his independent six-pack,
all questions cleansed

by the delicious freedom
of this moment.

The Men's Hour at the Local Grocery Store

At the small-town grocery store parking lot,
there was a lot more going on than just groceries
being piled into cars and carts being rounded up
by the evening crew. Here, the high school boys
carried on the proud tradition of being stockers and sackers
after school until they got off work at ten; then,
they rode the town hard for an hour each night
until the police shut them down. Now though,
it was only nine o'clock, and the lot was buzzing
with activity.

This was the men's hour at the local grocery store –
a chance for showing off a heavy stringer of catfish,
or the bloodied carcass of a recent kill –
a time for passing on knowledge to the younger generation –
where all the men were fathers,
and all the boys were sons.

So, on this night, even though anybody could see
that Jimbo's tie rod was shot to hell, still the men –
young, old, and older still — gathered round,
shining their flashlights to emphasize their points,
crawling around under the wrecked truck in the parking lot,
their overalls the same faded gray as the concrete,
like some kind of small-town chameleons
blending into their environment, oblivious
to the very real danger of being run over,
instead concerned entirely with the lesson of the moment –

a chance to show their sons
how men
respond to adversity.

Professor

The little professor, with her gray hair and one bad hip, wobbles
across the campus green to her next class, burdened
by the weight of her books. She has traveled this path
through political and economic upheavals, hurricanes
and earthquakes, her husband's death and her son's marriage –
yet she continues on her journey, committed
to fulfilling her duty.

Why does she do it – endure –
her burden, year after year?
She is tired, her body sore, her heart conflicted
with grief, yet she wobbles on – committed
to teaching her students what she knows about life, convicted
that humankind matters, that she is part
of the promise of humanity.

Corporate America

There are cameras in every corner, and ears on every
blank face decorating the hallways. Don't bother smiling
or saying hello. You're in Corporate America. Blink
once. Go on. Look busy and hurry away quickly. Be
blunt. Get to the point. Maximize time. Minimize life. Be
on call always. You belong to Corporate America.

No. "Corporate America": You can have it. Take it.
I'll take my own life, thank you. Commit Corporate Suicide.

I'll suck on the marrow of family dinners, laughter,
and weekends at the lake. I'll wipe my sopping chops
on fresh sheets hung in love on the line, dried by summer breezes.
I'll cultivate herds of happiness
to replace the ones I eat up in my healthy hunger
and quench my thirst with the same love
with which I'll water the herds.

Life should be fat and rich, and not by monetary reward.
Fatten me with what was worthy before the thought of money.
Fatten me with warmth and not cold metals.
Let me grow fat.

And take *that!*
you skinny, well-dressed, fashion-conscious men and women
of Corporate America!
Take *that!*
you mannequin look-alikes, with plastic minds to be molded
into whatever façade they demand of you!
Hard lines. Square lines.
Triangular, sharp lines.
Angles of knives.

Give me circles.
Give me down pillows to squeeze gleefully at night.
Give me orange suns and midnight moons.
Let my life be round, round and fat, and I will embrace it all
like a Whitmanesque angel!

Soft feathers, soft dreams, a soft flight out
of this god-forsaken skyscraper with elevators
running like cattle cars all day and all night.
I'll take my own life, thank you.
I'll commit Corporate Suicide.

You commit me to memory.
You wonder at my decision.
You gape at my audacity.
And somewhere in the darkest abysses of your being,
you envy me.
You envy my day off in the middle of the week,
my morning muffins, my ability to keep
evening plans and promises.

No one has the right to steal my life from me.
No one has the right to buy it.
I'll take my own life, thank you. I've seen yours.

I've seen your "top executive" time sheet: you,
the highest paid person in the company – you,
and your 80 hours a week. I've seen you.

And like a mother who wants to hide her child's shameful mess,
I want to diaper this malady and hide your shame,
but I'll not be powerless. I'll not be bought.
I'll not hide the shameful secrets of others,
and powder them up to smell fresh.
There's no disguising a rotting sickness,
the diarrhea of workaholics.

I pass by a man, probably brilliant, probably used-to-be-sane,
and he's sitting at a computer,
a photo of a black and white lily on the screen.
He sits there, music piped into his ears
by company-bought earplugs, wired to his computer,
his fingers poised above the keyboard
to give the appearance of working,
but all he is doing is watching the lily close.
Open and close. Open and close.

Let me stay open.
Let me bloom like a fragrant lily,
and not die an aching bud
at the onset of life.

There is a difference between onset and onslaught.
The difference is the slaughter, and those that are new
shed blood for those that are used up and bitter,
frigid, stiff, aching to live, and aching to die, just aching,
just bending over to totter on the edge of the grave,
grasping onto the living to pay more dues, put in more time,
earn their keep like they did before they broke.

And who deserves my dues? Who deserves my time?
Who deserves my life, my death, my aching back?
Who deserves to suckle my happiness dry?

Not you – you overdressed men choked by neckties.
Not you – you overworked women bound by pantyhose.
No, I think not.

I'll take my own life, thank you.

Jessica Isaacs is an English professor at Seminole State College, where she serves as the director of the annual Howlers & Yawpers Creativity Symposium.

She has presented her writing at several regional and national conferences. She has published her poems in various journals and anthologies, including *Cybersoleil Literary Journal, All Roads Lead Home Poetry Blog, SugarMule's Women Writing Nature, The Muse, Elegant Rage,* an audio book – *Spare Ashes,* and a chapbook – *smoldering embers.* She is a member of the coordinating committee for the Woody Guthrie Poets, and she is also the editor of *Dragon Poet Review & Quarterly,* an online literary journal and blog.

She makes her home in Prague, Oklahoma with her husband, kids, dogs, cats, and fish.